D1573364

MONSTER MANIA

MAGIC MONSTERS

FROM WITCHES TO GOBLINS

KATIE MARSICO

LERNER PUBLICATIONS ◆ MINNEAPOLIS

*Dedicated to Dylan, Ashlyn,
and Mabel Fergus*

Lerner Publications
A division of Lerner Publishing Group, Inc.
241 First Avenue North
Minneapolis, MN 55401 USA

For reading levels and more information, look up this title at www.lernerbooks.com.

Main body text set in Adrianna Regular 15/19.
Typeface provided by Chank.

Library of Congress Cataloging-in-Publication Data

Names: Marsico, Katie, 1980– author.
Title: Magic monsters : from witches to goblins / by Katie Marsico.
Description: Minneapolis : Lerner Publications, 2016. | Series: Monster mania | Includes
    bibliographical references and index.
Identifiers: LCCN 2016019520 (print) | LCCN 2016033424 (ebook) | ISBN 9781512425956 (lb :
    alk. paper) | ISBN 9781512428155 (eb pdf)
Subjects: LCSH: Witches—Juvenile literature. | Magic—Juvenile literature. | Goblins—Juvenile
    literature.
Classification: LCC BF1566 .M29455 2016 (print) | LCC BF1566 (ebook) | DDC 133.4—dc23

LC record available at https://lccn.loc.gov/2016019520

Manufactured in the United States of America
1-41363-23307-8/1/2016

CONTENTS

COME TO THE CAULDRON!

A witch brews her magical potion.

A witch bends over a bubbling cauldron. Steam rises past her green, wrinkled face. As she stirs her brew, her lips move. She's chanting a spell! What potion is she making?

Maybe you've read scenes like this in fairy tales. In some tales, witches and wizards have special powers. They use their powers to do magic. Witches and wizards may look a lot like humans. But tales about their dark skills make them seem more like monsters.

There are other magical monsters too. Goblins also do magic. In some stories, goblins are shape-shifters. They can change the shape of their bodies.

Stories about magical monsters have been told for years. Yet they are still a big part of modern tales. Are these beings real or imaginary? Amusing or evil? Decide for yourself! But first, prepare to explore myths—and the mystery of magic!

CHAPTER ONE
MAKING MYTHS

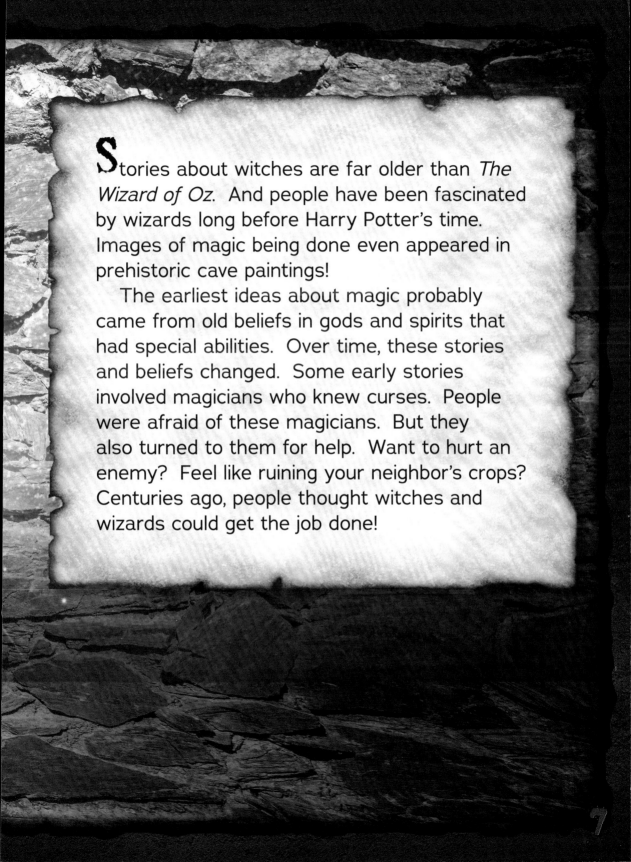

Stories about witches are far older than *The Wizard of Oz*. And people have been fascinated by wizards long before Harry Potter's time. Images of magic being done even appeared in prehistoric cave paintings!

The earliest ideas about magic probably came from old beliefs in gods and spirits that had special abilities. Over time, these stories and beliefs changed. Some early stories involved magicians who knew curses. People were afraid of these magicians. But they also turned to them for help. Want to hurt an enemy? Feel like ruining your neighbor's crops? Centuries ago, people thought witches and wizards could get the job done!

Medieval Magicians

By medieval times, ideas about magic had grown scarier. Storytellers often described witches as toothless old women. Wizards were often shown in robes. Many also wore a cone-shaped hat and had a wand. People thought witches could fly. They could control weather and cause storms too. Some could become wolves or rabbits. Others could make themselves invisible.

Stories about magicians' skills were fascinating. But witches and wizards were often seen as evil. Some people thought the devil gave them their powers. People said to be witches or wizards could be put in jail or even killed!

From Crude to Clever

Medieval legends told of goblins too. Storytellers described them as ugly fairies. But not all goblins were identical. Many were short and hairy. Some were like elves. Others looked like mermaids. In some stories, goblins loved gold. Most were harmless and liked playing jokes. But some were dangerous. They made people have accidents. Goblins called knockers even made mines cave in!

Goblins found their way into fairy tales. Does the word *rumpelstilt* sound familiar? A rumpelstilt is a noisy goblin. The story of Rumpelstiltskin dates back to nineteenth-century Germany. Rumpelstiltskin is a goblin-like creature who uses magic to spin straw into gold.

The fairy tale creature Rumpelstiltskin helps a young girl spin straw into gold.

In southwestern Asia, people told stories of other magical creatures called jinn. Ancient wizards trapped these spirits in magical lamps and bottles. Jinn used their powers to grant three wishes to whoever helped them escape. Later, jinn became known as genies.

Left to right: Evie, Carlos, Mal, and Jay are characters in Disney Channel's *Descendants*.

CHAPTER TWO
EVERYDAY MAGIC

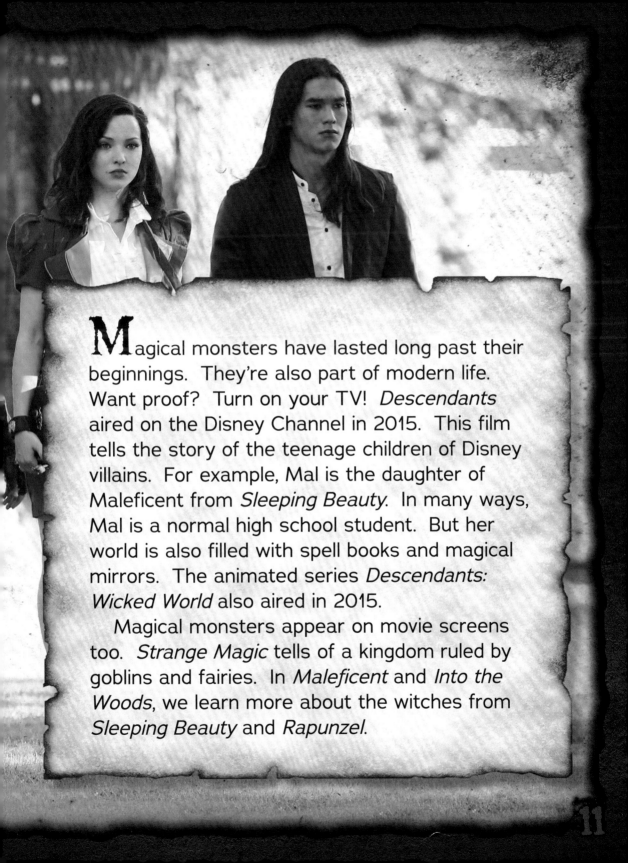

Magical monsters have lasted long past their beginnings. They're also part of modern life. Want proof? Turn on your TV! *Descendants* aired on the Disney Channel in 2015. This film tells the story of the teenage children of Disney villains. For example, Mal is the daughter of Maleficent from *Sleeping Beauty*. In many ways, Mal is a normal high school student. But her world is also filled with spell books and magical mirrors. The animated series *Descendants: Wicked World* also aired in 2015.

Magical monsters appear on movie screens too. *Strange Magic* tells of a kingdom ruled by goblins and fairies. In *Maleficent* and *Into the Woods*, we learn more about the witches from *Sleeping Beauty* and *Rapunzel*.

Fans of magical movies also know the *Lord of the Rings* trilogy. In these films, wizards, goblins, and other creatures are all part of a quest to destroy a powerful ring.

Spellbinding Books and Comics

Many films about magical monsters began as books. The *Lord of the Rings* trilogy is based on books by J. R. R. Tolkien. And before Harry Potter came to theaters, he appeared in books by J. K. Rowling. Harry and his friends attend Hogwarts School of Witchcraft and Wizardry. Their education involves magic wands and flying broomsticks!

Comic books also feature magical characters. Scarlet Witch is a figure in Marvel comics.

Elizabeth Olsen played Scarlet Witch in the 2016 movie *Captain America: Civil War.*

She's able to change reality and even creates a new world. DC Comics has several magicians too, including Weather Wizard. He uses his wand to control blizzards and lightning bolts.

From Toys to Sports Teams

Magical creatures don't just exist in books and movies. Toy companies make magical monsters too. Lego figures include witches and wizards. Mattel's Monster High dolls include the witch Casta Fierce and her genie friend, Gigi Grant.

Magical creatures also appear in the board game *Small World*. Players compete to build empires with sorcerers, wizards, goblins, and other creatures. Similar characters are found in the games *Dungeons & Dragons* and *Minecraft*.

Magical monsters can even be found on sports teams! The Washington Wizards are a professional basketball team. And magical Irish elves are often seen at University of Notre Dame (UND) games. Can you guess which creature you'll find on UND sportswear? A leprechaun!

The Wicked Witch of the West from *The Wizard of Oz* is one of the most famous witches.

WHAT DO YOU THINK?

Think about the movie *The Wizard of Oz.* Maybe you've also seen the musical *Wicked.* How about *The Wiz?* They all have similar characters and stories. And they all feature both good and bad witches. What's magical about the good witches? How about the bad witches? Whose magic do you think is stronger? Why?

Jemma Rix plays the wicked witch Elphaba in a production of *Wicked.*

CHAPTER THREE
FACT OR FANTASY?

People who created
medicines from plants often
had shops to sell their
mixtures and ingredients.

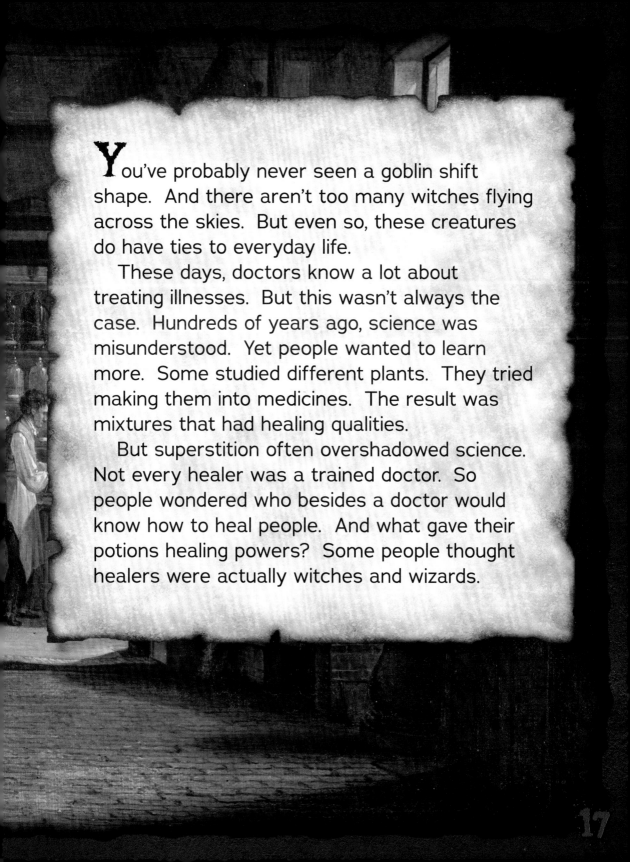

You've probably never seen a goblin shift shape. And there aren't too many witches flying across the skies. But even so, these creatures do have ties to everyday life.

These days, doctors know a lot about treating illnesses. But this wasn't always the case. Hundreds of years ago, science was misunderstood. Yet people wanted to learn more. Some studied different plants. They tried making them into medicines. The result was mixtures that had healing qualities.

But superstition often overshadowed science. Not every healer was a trained doctor. So people wondered who besides a doctor would know how to heal people. And what gave their potions healing powers? Some people thought healers were actually witches and wizards.

Who's a Magical Monster?

It didn't always take much to be labeled a monster. Sometimes seeming "magical" was as simple as standing out in a crowd. During the 1690s, some women in Salem, Massachusetts, were accused of witchcraft. These women often had a few things in common. Most were more outspoken than their neighbors. Many were poor, widows, or childless. These women didn't fit popular ideas about what was "normal" in their communities.

This scene shows a witchcraft trial in Salem, Massachusetts.

Myths of other magical creatures may have formed the same way. Modern scientists understand genetics. They know what causes certain physical features. Yet in the past, looking different from others could be dangerous. People thought a unique appearance came from magic. For example, maybe what people thought were goblins and leprechauns were actually humans. Maybe they just weren't identical to the people around them!

Leprechauns in stories are often clever shoemakers that can grant wishes.

Lights, Camera, Action!

A woman in Argentina claimed she had proof goblins are real! She said that in 2011 she had videotaped a goblin running across her kitchen. Thanks to social media, her video spread like wildfire. And her video isn't the only one of its kind. Others claim to have evidence of magical monsters too.

Doubters say these images are tricks. Photos and videos can be edited to show something that isn't real. People might create false proof of magical creatures to gain money or fame. Yet some people think magical monsters are more than myths. These people don't think every piece of evidence is fake. And even if it is, maybe better proof will one day be found!

MAPPING MAGIC

Most nations have their own twist on magical monsters. Filipino stories talk about *nunos*. These goblins are said to live in anthills or termite mounds. They spit on anyone who disturbs their homes. Their saliva is said to cause pain and sickness.

On the other side of the world, people in the southwestern United States tell stories of skinwalkers. In Navajo legends, skinwalkers are witches. They look human during the day. But at night, they change into animals. Skinwalkers may appear as coyotes, owls, foxes, wolves, or crows.

Meanwhile, beware of *biloko* in the forests of the African country the Democratic Republic of the Congo! These goblins have claws and snouts. Grass grows on their bodies. Biloko are cruel and cast spells on people.

In Navajo stories, a skinwalker might appear as an owl or other animal.

CHAPTER FOUR
TIMELESS TALES

Disney first made the story *The Sword in the Stone* into a movie in 1963.

Tales about magical monsters are here to stay! Disney plans to release *Descendants 2* in 2017. And people continue breathing fresh life into old stories. According to Disney, a new movie about genies is being made. Filmmakers are remaking *The Sword in the Stone* too. This tale focuses on King Arthur's boyhood. His friendship with the wizard Merlin is a big part of the story.

Social media is also important to the future of magical monsters. The Internet lets people share information quickly. Remember those magical cave paintings? They're a mouse click away. So are myths about witches from around the world. You can even find goblin videos online!

Fear and Fascination

Sometimes modern science reshapes magical myths. Medical research is no longer seen as magical. People usually don't think witches control weather. And compared to medieval times, fewer cultures fear curses.

Will attitudes toward magical

Before they understood modern medicine, doctors thought that wearing a mask filled with herbs would keep them healthy.

creatures eventually change? It's hard to tell.
Myths about witches, wizards, and goblins
often spark fear. But they also fuel a timeless
fascination with magic.

Stories of spooky witches and magical potions continue
to fascinate people of all ages.

GOBLIN

SIZE
Usually small, about 12 inches (30 centimeters) tall

MAGICAL POWERS
Has the ability to shape-shift, become invisible, and transform matter (for example, spinning straw into gold)

OTHER TRAITS
Often sly and greedy, known for both helping and harming humans

GOOD OR EVIL?
Both

LIKELY TO WIN OR LOSE
Likely to lose

JINN/GENIE

SIZE
Varies (depending on whether it is trapped and on the form it takes when freed since it can appear as a human or an animal)

MAGICAL POWERS
Has the ability to shape-shift and grant wishes

OTHER TRAITS
Very smart and cunning, known for both helping and harming humans

GOOD OR EVIL?
Both

LIKELY TO WIN OR LOSE
Likely to win

27

GLOSSARY

cauldron: a large metal pot for cooking over an open fire

conjure: to make something appear unexpectedly, as if by magic

curse: words that call upon a supernatural power to harm someone

genetics: the study of how certain characteristics are passed from one generation to the next

identical: exactly the same

medieval: describing the Middle Ages (about 500–1500)

superstition: a belief founded on ideas involving supernatural forces, rather than science

trilogy: a series of three books or movies that are closely related and have the same characters or themes

Books

Cox, Barbara, and Scott Forbes. *Witches, Wizards, and Dark Magic.* New York: Gareth Stevens, 2014.

Pearson, Maggie, and Francesca Greenwood. *Ghosts and Goblins: Scary Stories from around the World.* Minneapolis: Darby Creek, 2016.

Waxman, Laura Hamilton. *Who Were the Accused Witches of Salem? And Other Questions about the Witchcraft Trials.* Minneapolis: Lerner Publications, 2012.

Movies

Fantastic Beasts and Where to Find Them. Directed by David Yates. London: Heyday Films, 2016.

Maleficent. Directed by Robert Stromberg. Burbank, CA: Walt Disney Pictures, 2014.

Strange Magic. Directed by Gary Rydstrom. San Francisco: Lucasfilm, 2015.

TV Shows

Descendants: Wicked World. Broadcast on Disney Channel, 2015–.

Once upon a Time. Broadcast on ABC, 2011–.

Winx Club. Italian television series, broadcast worldwide, 2004–.

Video Games

Book of Potions. Video game. London: SCE London Studio, 2013.

Lego: The Hobbit. Video game. Cheshire, UK: Traveller's Tales, 2014.

Magic Touch: Wizard for Hire. Video game. London: Nitrome, 2015.

Websites

The Harry Potter Lexicon—Wizards, Witches and Beings
http://www.hp-lexicon.org/gate/characters.html

History for Kids—Myths and Legends
http://www.history-for-kids.com/myths-and-legends.html

National Geographic Kids—"The Salem Witch Trials"
http://kids.nationalgeographic.com/explore/history/the
-salem-witch-trials/

INDEX

PHOTO ACKNOWLEDGMENTS

The images in this book are used with the permission of: backgrounds throughout: © iStockphoto.com/Lynne Yoshii (burnt parchment); © iStockphoto.com/konradlew (paper edge frame); © iStockphoto.com/STILLFX (red wall background); © iStockphoto.com/South_agency, p. 1 (eyeball); © iStockphoto.com/Natalia Lukiyanova, pp. 1, 2 (monster claws); © iStockphoto.com/dmilovanovic, pp. 2–3 (ripped paper edge); © Marcin Sylwia Ciesielski/Shutterstock.com, pp. 4–5; © BrunoGarridoMacias/Shutterstock.com, pp. 6–7; © VeraPetruk/iStock/Thinkstock, pp. 8–9 (candle background); © Ernest Mister/Bridgeman Images, p. 9 (inset); © Jack Rowand/Disney Channel/Getty Images, pp. 10–11; © Marvel Studios/Kobal Collection/Art Resource, NY, p. 12; © Remy/iStock/Thinkstock, pp. 12–13 (background); Mary Evans/Ronald Grant/WARNER BROS MGM/Courtesy Everett Collection, pp. 14–15; © Scott Barbour/Getty Images, p. 15 (inset); © Everett/Shutterstock.com, pp. 16–17; © Niday Picture Library/Alamy, p. 18; © kirstypargeter/iStock/Thinkstock, pp. 18–19 (background); Warner Bros./Kobal Collection/Art Resource, NY, p. 19; © iStockphoto.com/DNY59, pp. 20–21 (background); © Ondrej Prosicky/Shutterstock.com, p. 21; Walt Disney Pictures/Courtesy Everett Collection, pp. 22–23; © Falkensteinfoto/Alamy, p. 24; © Gewoldi/iStock/Thinkstock, pp. 24–25 (background); © Kiselev Andrey Valerevich/Shutterstock.com, p. 25; © iStockphoto.com/AVTG, pp. 26–27 (background); © chorazin3d/Dreamstime.com, p. 26; © iStockphoto.com/Ruslan_Kokarev, p. 27;

Cover: © iStockphoto.com/olegkalina (night sky); © iStockphoto.com/79govinda, (witch silhouette); © kristypargeter/iStock/Thinkstock (full moon and tree); © iStockphoto.com/South_agency (eyeball); © iStockphoto.com/Natalia Lukiyanova (monster claws); © iStockphoto.com/Lynne Yoshii (burnt parchment); © iStockphoto.com/STILLFX (red wall background).